For our grandchildren, Zoë and Dylan.

May they come to love the game as we do.

MH & GG

First published by Ford Street Publishing,
162 Hoddle Street, Abbotsford,
Melbourne Victoria Australia

2 4 6 8 10 9 7 5 3 1

First published 2020

National Library of Australia Cataloguing-in-Publication entry:
Authors: Gloury, Gabrielle; Hyde, Michael
Title: Girls Change the Game / Gabrielle Gloury & Michael Hyde

ISBN: 9781925804492 (paperback)

A catalogue record for this book is available from the National Library of Australia

Text design: © Grant Gittus Graphics
Cover design: Cathy Larsen Design
In-house editors: Abigail Cini & Robyn Donoghue
Illustration and design © copyright 2006 Hardie Grant Egmont
Printed in Australia by McPherson's Printing Group

Aussie Rules

by

GABRIELLE GLOURY
MICHAEL HYDE

FORD ST

Westpark Scorpions

Westpark Scorpions Under 14 Girls Football Team

A Champion Team can always beat a Team of Champions.

Coach: Brenda Cross

Runner: Andy Meredith

Manager/Medico: Anna Trung

Player Positions:

Backs:	Hannah	Isabella	Beth
Half Backs:	Holly	Chandra	Matilda
Centre:	Sophie		
Half Forwards:	Ava	Grace	Ruby
Forwards:	Zoe	Talia	Thao
Followers:	Heidi	Emma	Elly
Interchange:	Poppy, Bec, Ivy, Jasmine		

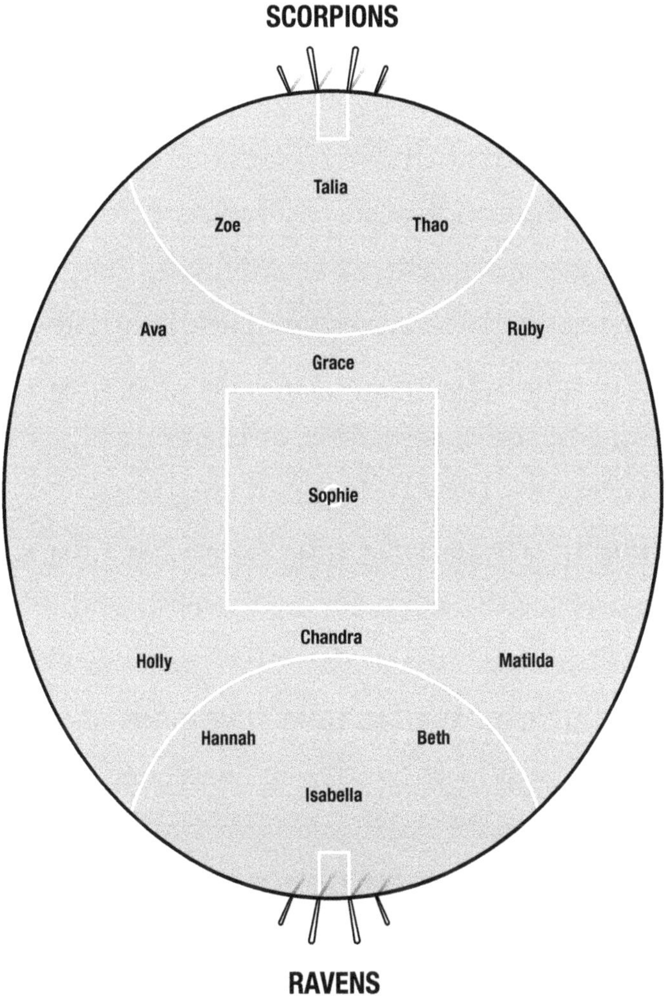

SCORPIONS

Talia

Zoe Thao

Ava Ruby

Grace

Sophie

Chandra

Holly Matilda

Hannah Beth

Isabella

RAVENS

PLAY BEGINS

The Scorpions Under 14 Girls line-up had just been announced two nights before – with great excitement and delight. They are the first girls' team of Westpark Football Club and here they are in their very first game of the competition at the start of a brand new season. It was a long time coming. There had been a lot of hard work done over the last year by the club and parents to establish the girls' team. Weekly training over the summer had made them fit and taught them the skills needed to play at this level. Hours of drills and rehearsing set plays helped the Scorpions prepare for competition. They needed this because they are up against the in-form and established team of the Girls Under 14 Division, the Eastvale Ravens, who won the premiership the previous season. The Scorpions are bursting with nervous excitement.

Players, parents, big and little brothers and sisters, friends and some who had missed out on selection, pack the change room. Club President, Stephanie Pellegrino, stands proudly watching. The coach, Brenda Cross, wanders around the room, having a quiet word with each of the girls. Team Manager Anna Trung checks the girls' nails. The players know that earrings and jewellery are not allowed, but Anna checks for them as well. Nasty injuries had sometimes occurred when players forgot to take them out.

Coach Brenda has a face-to-face chat with the Captain, Zoe, who smiles in response. Zoe has been a popular choice as Captain. She is supportive of her teammates and keeps a level head; not easily swept up by what was happening on the field.

The coach moves around the room, nods and smiles at Ivy, her daughter, but says nothing. It isn't a good idea to pay too much attention to Ivy. You have to be careful about these things when you are coach, otherwise there'd be complaints about favouritism. The same problem lay with Andy, the club's runner, and his daughter and ruck extraordinaire, Heidi.

Isabella sits by herself, chewing her nails, jiggling her feet – something she does before every practice game. Isabella nervously glances at her grandmother, Lizzie. She is near the door, sitting in her wheelchair, breathing on a tube connected to her oxygen tank. Lizzie has been sick for a long time. Thanks to Isabella's mum, Lizzie attended every training session and now she will see her granddaughter play in a real competition game.

Twins, Ava and Poppy, the youngest on the team and usually inseparable, braid each other's hair – something that their first coach, Norm Healy, never allowed. Norm thought this distracted the girls from the task at hand. He was a tough old coach, generous with his time, but an accident at his work forced him to bow out while he recovered. After a lengthy search, Brenda came on board and changed a number of things. She saw keeping the girls relaxed helped them focus. However, Brenda had stopped them using their phones before the game. In fact, she made them put their phones into an old supermarket bag that she personally took around the room. 'Texts, Instagram and Snapchat et cetera are all okay after a game but not before. Focus and concentration. We're either serious or we're not!'

Chandra, Holly and Talia are at the

end of the room, practising their short kicking. Others listen to the music playing in the rooms while checking their mouthguards and boots. Bec, the eldest and most experienced girl on the team, looks on. She'd played in a mixed comp down the coast and came to the Scorpions a year ago when her family moved to this side of town. Emma's knees were being taped up. She'd had trouble with them when she played basketball. The same with Elly's right ankle, which gave her strife over the years of playing soccer. Even with these physical weaknesses they both much preferred to play footy.

There is tension in the room with everybody doing their best to keep on track. Even Matilda's dad Joe, famous for his encouragement and bellowing roars of support, manages to stay quiet, much to the relief of his daughter. Parents could be so embarrassing.

Andy, the runner, puts his fingers to his lips for his famous piercing whistle and calls the team together to listen to the last few instructions from Coach Brenda. The girls gather in a tight circle, arms around each other.

'Girls.' Brenda has lost her smile. She is all business now. 'Girls, today is more than a footy game. It's the day our footy club launches its first girls' team. It's our first game and I'd be kidding you if I didn't say that our opposition, the Ravens, are one of the toughest in our league. They're a skilled bunch and we'll have to be on top of our game to have any chance. Get rid of your nerves by getting into the game at your earliest chance. Everybody has to put in. We don't want anybody relying on some of our hard running players like Elly and Talia. Sure they're good, we all know that, but we'd be nothing if it weren't for Beth's tackles, Sophie's long runs or Heidi's hit-outs. Remember our club slogan: "A champion team can always beat a team of champions".'

The girls start to become restless. After all, it is their first competition game and they are up against an experienced team with a number of brilliant players, like their Centre, Maddy, a gun midfielder who won the Best and Fairest last season. Rose, the super strong Ravens ruck, is also known to some of the Scorpions from the days of learning the game in primary school. No wonder the Scorpions are restless; they just want to get out there and play.

'Okay!' Brenda shouts. 'One last thing. You've done the hard work, now let's see it in action. If you make a mistake, I don't want anybody hanging their heads like I've seen some of the boys doing. You get straight back into the game. And remember, if the umpire's call doesn't go your way, there's to be no arguing. The umpire is always right. Play hard and fair. All right, all hands in!'

The team bunches together and yells, ***'SCORPIONS!!'***

As Zoe leads them out onto the ground, even the biggest diehard fans would've been shocked at the roar, the yelling, the chanting, the applause, the tooting of car horns from what seemed like a crowd of hundreds. The girls burst through their first banner painted with a huge bright red scorpion on a yellow background emblazoned with the words: ***Scorpions Girls Change the Game***

The ground is quite firm, which allows for a running game. But one of the girls points at the sky where some menacing dark grey clouds loom. 'Might end up pretty wet and muddy!' yells

Hannah, who is well known for her love of playing in mud and rain.

The team glances at their opposition who are already out on the ground, looking fit and ready to go. Zoe directs the team to one end of the ground to do their sprints and a bit of kicking for goal. The crowd has swelled. Parents nervously gather together and some find things to do like help Anna organise the First Aid kit or cut up the oranges. Chandra's dad goes off to help Joe with the sausage sizzle – the smell covers the ground.

The umpire calls Zoe and the Ravens' captain to the centre for the coin toss. As it spins into the air, Zoe calls 'tails' and down it comes.

'Heads,' the umpire calls.

Not the best start, Zoe thinks, as she runs back to her team of Scorpions.

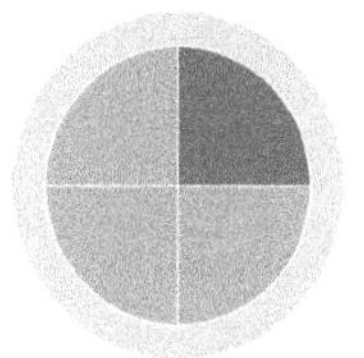

FIRST QUARTER

The teams move into position. There's a bit of shoving and pushing going on. Clearly there's a lot of feeling in this game. Zoe adjusts her mouthguard and Emma tightens the strap on her helmet. Ever since she had a bad stack on her skateboard, her parents insisted she wear a helmet in all sports. She taps the top of her helmet twice for good luck. The siren sounds. The umpire blows her whistle and we're away in the first official game for the Scorpions. We're about to see just how good this team is when up against the reigning champions. The crowd has come from miles around to see this game, and boy, are they looking forward to it.

It's the first bounce of the game. Heidi is in the ruck and leaps like a gazelle to win the first hit-out. The footy comes straight down to former soccer star, Elly. It was doubtful as to whether she'd be able to play this week since her ankle had been troublesome. She runs off and kicks wildly – right into the safe hands of the Ravens' defence. That's usually what happens to hurried kicks. A Ravens half back handballs over the top to a running on-baller who is away with plenty of clear space ahead. But Sophie, the speedster Scorpions midfielder, puts on the burners, placing pressure on the Ravens player who still gets her kick away to the running lead of the Ravens' forward, Kaitlyn. She doesn't hesitate, runs around Hannah's grasping hands and snaps a goal!

First goal to the Ravens, and to be truthful, some of the Scorpions look shell-shocked. They're going to have to pick up their game if they don't want to be blown away.

Back in the centre, Andy takes messages to Emma and Elly. Coach Brenda wants them to apply more pressure right from the get-go. Emma is more of the inside player who has to work harder around the ball. The umpire bounces the ball but it goes off on an angle and is recalled. She throws it up and Heidi jumps as if she has wings, bringing the footy down to Emma. Elly collects Emma's handball and is immediately tackled and gives away a free. Playing the real thing sure is harder than practice matches. Once again, the Ravens are away through the corridor. There's a fast handball to Maddy, their slick on-baller, who dodges and weaves.

But Chandra and Elly are onto her, desperate to lay a tackle.

First Decision Point:

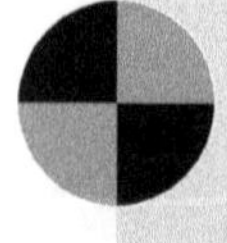

Do Chandra and Elly successfully tackle Maddy, the Ravens player?

Go to page 21

OR

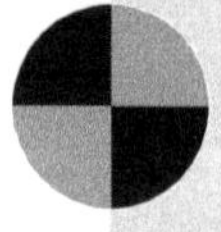

Does Maddy, the Ravens player, escape the tackle from Chandra and Elly?

Go to page 31

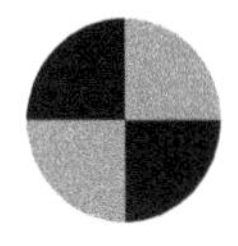

You decided that Chandra and Elly successfully tackle the Ravens player.

Chandra and Elly solidly wrap Maddy in a huge tackle, stopping her in her tracks. Both Scorpions struggle for the ball. Maddy hits the deck, but somehow knocks the footy away to a teammate who scuffs a kick and the ball rolls over the boundary line, ten metres from the Ravens' goal. Chandra yells to the umpire that it was an intentional out of bounds.

'Nothing doing,' says the umpire.

Elly keeps on with the argument. 'C'mon ump. It was obvious.' The umpire cautions Elly and Chandra. They better stop now because it will cost them big-time if they don't and Brenda has often reminded the girls that the umpire is always right.

Throw-in and the ball gets wrapped

up in a tangle of bodies. The ball goes out of bounds yet again. Dangerous time for the Scorpions with the play being only 15 metres out from the Ravens' goal. All that's required is a quick kick out of the pack by the Ravens for them to score. Isabella drops back in the square. Good thinking! She's a thinker that girl; pays attention to detail and loves her footy.

The boundary umpire gets ready for a throw-in. Heidi works into a good position to get the hit-out. She taps the ball down, there's a strangle of hands, ball bobbling around. The Ravens on-baller somehow finds the footy and snaps a goal from nowhere. How she found space in that crowd is amazing! Unfortunately for the Scorpions, it's another goal to the Ravens while they have yet to worry the scoreboard. It must be the first quarter nerves.

Only a few minutes to go till quarter-time. The Scorpions need to get a hurry-on if they're going to have anything to show for their first quarter of big-time football.

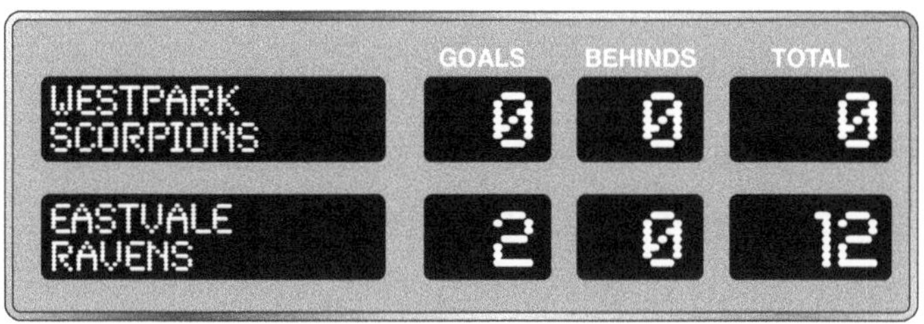

This time, the umpire throws the ball up and neither of the rucks can get an advantage. Emma is at it on the ground with another four players trying to wrest the ball out. A Ravens player grabs the ball, but only for a second, as Emma strips it from her and fires a bullet-like handpass to Matilda, who has bravely left her opponent. She gathers and passes it backwards to Holly who then switches play with a big, big kick. Thao, who's moved up the ground, makes a desperate effort to collect the footy.

With protection from Talia, Thao manages to handball to Elly – a brave effort considering how many Ravens near the forward line were coming for her. Elly passes it to Zoe who kicks across her body and . . . it hits the post! Well at least it's a score for the Scorpions. And the siren sounds for quarter-time.

The girls wolf down oranges, gulp drinks and a few get into the snakes. Coach Brenda and team manager, Anna, aren't too keen on the lollies, but the girls reckon it gives them a boost. Anna has argued that it all goes away after ten minutes and they end up feeling flatter than before. Never mind. They let it go.

Captain Zoe apologises for kicking a behind, but the others tell her not to worry about it. 'I'll get it next time,' she promises. Coach takes the forwards aside in a separate bunch. Ava, Grace, Ruby, Zoe, Talia and Thao look worried.

'It's okay, girls,' says Brenda. 'Just a few quick reminders. These Ravens know how to play and you'll notice that they're not going to give you half a second in our forward 50. You're going to need slick hands and take any opportunity. If you have the chance to kick, lower your eyes and pick a target. Just remember the drills we did over summer. All of you are accurate kickers. Talia, you're the tallest girl in the forward 50, so use your height to your advantage. Go for your marks and if you don't get it, their backs will just as likely chop your arms and you'll get a free anyway.'

The forwards rejoin the group.

'All right, all hands in!'

The team bunches together and yells, ***'SCORPIONS!!'***

SECOND QUARTER

Ball's bounced. Up it goes. This time, Heidi is clearly beaten by the Ravens' ruck, Rose, who is built like a tank and out-muscles Heidi. Strong and athletic, she brings the ball down to her on-ballers who seem to have entered this second quarter as though they have something to prove. The Ravens are the team to beat and are determined to win against the newcomers. It seems like that last behind from the Scorpions has urged the Ravens on!

The Ravens' forward finds a gap in the Scorpions' defence and fires out a handpass to a running teammate. She's off with Hannah hot on her tail. This move looks dangerous for the Scorpions' backline as the ball is bombed long into the Ravens forwards. It lands 20 metres out from the Ravens' goal. Ivy, who's come off the bench to replace Poppy, tracks the ball and traps it with amazing skill for such a young player. She takes one bounce, runs backwards, swivels, bounces again. She's looking for space. She's fast this girl. Isabella is on offer, but Ivy doesn't see the Ravens bearing down on her and she's brought to ground. No free kick either way, but never mind because Ivy stopped an almost inevitable goal. Again, a throw-up.

The footy lands dangerously close to the Ravens' goal. Despite a huge leap, Heidi misses the ball and friendly fire from the Scorpions' ruck takes out Beth who was waiting for the ball. Beth's a tough cookie and gets to her feet. Now Matilda, reading the situation, makes the brave decision to leave her direct opponent and goes in to get the loose ball.

There's another pack forming. Courage wins the day as Matilda goes in for a second and third attempt and comes out with the ball. In desperation, she manages a short kick to Ruby.

The Scorpions are putting up a great defence. Can the Scorps turn defence into attack? The Ravens try to corral Ruby, who takes on a tackler. Can she get through this wall of Ravens? Ruby makes a HUUUGE kick into the Scorpions' forward line. No lowering of the eyes there. Bodies lunge. Lots of bodies are desperate for the ball. It's a Scorps' mark! Wow and wow! Talia emerges with the ball. Looks like Zoe copped a whack in there. She gingerly gets to her feet and has a few quiet words to Talia who lines up for goal.

Second Decision Point:

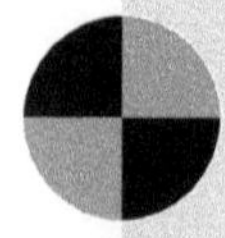

Does Talia kick the goal?

Go to page  40

OR

Does Talia miss an easy goal?

Go to page  47

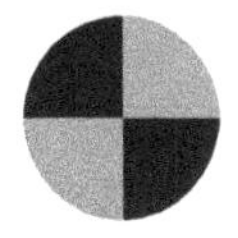

You decided that Maddy, the Ravens player, escapes the tackle from Chandra and Elly.

Chandra and Elly are working hard to stop Maddy and they succeed in tackling her to the ground. Maddy twists one way, then the other and breaks the tackle, slips, and as she does, manages to get boot to ball. The ball is still on the ground, rolling this way and that. It could still go through for a goal or it could roll out of bounds. Hold your breath. No goal, but she manages a behind. Ravens are disappointed and Scorpions breathe a sigh of relief.

	GOALS	BEHINDS	TOTAL
WESTPARK SCORPIONS	0	0	0
EASTVALE RAVENS	1	1	7

The Scorpions' full back, Isabella, wastes no time and kicks out to Beth, who's made good position deep in defence, 25 metres out from the Ravens' goal. She handballs on to Matilda running past who does a short, low kick to Sophie. She doesn't waste time either, handballing over the top of Ravens midfielders to Talia who has moved right up the ground. The Scorpions are playing a possession game. Talia drops back, looking for what's up forward. She touches the ball to the ground, runs backwards, then sees space and a target in the 50-metre arc. She kicks long, hard and direct to Jasmine, who's just come off the interchange bench. Jasmine's on a lead and clunks the mark 25 metres out at a 45-degree angle. This girl can kick. She's been playing on mixed teams since she was eight so she's not afraid of moments like this. Jasmine has a funny run-up, not straight or direct. Instead, she runs out to her right, comes back to her left and then kicks.

Off it goes, no worries there. It is the first goal for the Westpark Scorpions! Not only in this game, but their first goal as a new team in this Girls Comp. Well done! Needless to say the Scorp supporters have gone absolutely ballistic. Horns toot and chants of '*Scorpions, Scorpions*' resound around the ground. And the siren goes for the end of the first quarter.

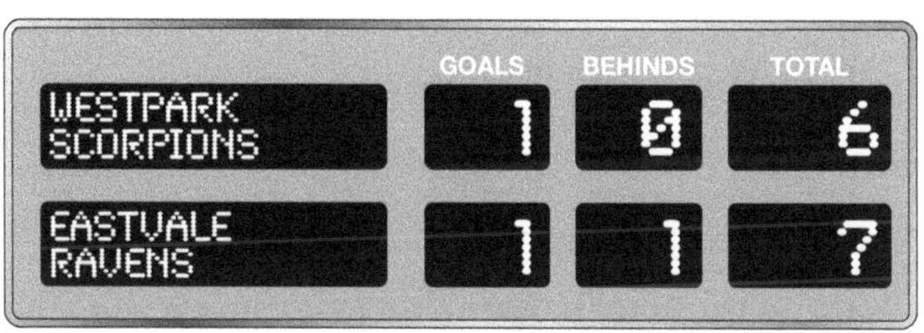

The Scorpions gather in the middle of the ground, water bottles in hand. Joe pats all of the girls on the back. Matilda is relieved that her dad has finally stopped cheering. She loves his support but could do without his bellowing yells of encouragement. Anna checks out Chandra and Elly who both received heavy knocks trying to stop the Ravens when they scored that last behind. Isabella has a nice little shiner that's come up, but she's a player who always says she's okay. Her grandmother, Lizzie, has been wheeled out onto the ground to hear the coach's quarter-time speech.

'Okay girls, gather round.' Andy tells them to shoosh up. 'Heidi, you're going well in the ruck. You've beaten Rose. She'll be annoyed at getting beaten, so keep at her. Also watch out for that leg she sticks out in front of her. Back six – well done. We'd be further behind if it weren't for your efforts. Chandra and Elly, very good work! And the play that led to that goal by Jasmine –' lots of 'Well done Jaz' comes from the others – 'from the backline to Talia, who didn't lose her head, all the way to our forwards. We need to see more of that. Keep the ball moving. The Ravens are super experienced and we need to keep them on their toes. First quarter is over and you've done really well. All right, hands in.'

'SCORPIONS!!' The team gears up for the next quarter.

SECOND QUARTER

The Scorpions have come out looking more confident after that goal. They know now that they can take it to the best team in the comp. Zoe reminds her teammates to concentrate. It's easy to let things ease off after a goal, but that's when experienced teams can take advantage.

Heidi remembers the Coach's timely warning about the Ravens' ruck sticking her foot straight out. Heidi's lucky she didn't cop it right in her breadbasket. This time, the Ravens win the hit-out but it's stolen by Sophie who is back in the centre. A Ravens follower is on her tail. She uses her speed, well-known to the Scorpions, but not to the opposition. Sophie puts on the burners, arches her back and accelerates away, leaving

Ravens players grasping for air. Sophie takes a tight turn as more Ravens descend on her. They almost catch her, but she turns on a dime and handballs to Ruby who sees a very open goal square and goes for it. But wait, Sophie's gone down, clutching her right knee. Doesn't look good. It's what can happen when your legs and centre are off balance. Meanwhile, Ruby has gone on to kick a big goal! The Scorpions run from all over the ground to congratulate her while others go to Sophie who is still lying on the ground, clutching her knee.

The crowd's attention is on Sophie who writhes in agony. The umpire stops play as the stretcher is called for. It could be a strain, but it could be much worse. The girls gather around her, looking worried. It might mean no more games this season. Those in the crowd look concerned as she's carried off the ground. Sophie's mum and stepdad have already brought the car up and she'll be off to hospital for scans. Brenda asks Sophie's mum to call her when they know more.

Second Decision Point:

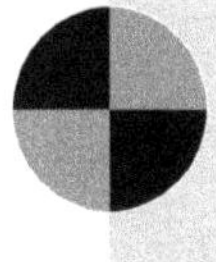

Does Coach Brenda choose her daughter, the fast-running Ivy, to take Sophie's place in the Centre?

Go to page  53

OR

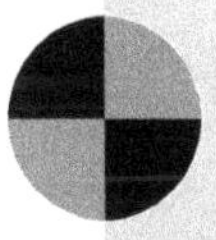

Does Coach Brenda choose the very experienced Bec to take Sophie's place in the Centre?

Go to page 63

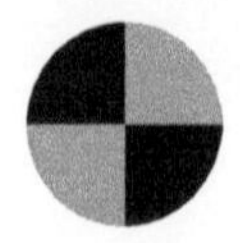

You decided that Talia kicks the goal.

This could be an historic first goal for the Scorpions so there's a bit of pressure on Talia here! From only 20 out, Talia sends the ball long and straight as a die, right through the middle. The goal umpire doesn't move as the beautiful kick sails through and nearly takes out the BBQ. The crowd laughs and Matilda's dad was the only one with his eye on the ball, marking it before the ball was barbecued!

Scorpions pile onto Talia for scoring their very first goal in the competition – the first of what they hope will be many. Scorpions all over the ground pump the air and the forwards give huge hugs and high-fives to Talia – their first goal-kicker in the comp. Looks like the coach's advice worked. Talia used her height to her advantage to take the mark and the

Scorpions scored a goal! A real triumph.

The Scorpions have their tails up. Heidi moves into place for the bounce. Zoe, Thao and Emma are making sure they're not pushed out of the fight for the ball. After a perfect bounce by the umpire, Ravens get a clear hit-out to their runners, but their half forward can't control the ball. She keeps tapping it forward, hoping for the right bounce. It tumbles, and the Ravens overrun it. Bit clumsy in their control of the footy. The Scorpions aren't letting up for a minute. Poppy, small but agile, sees her chance. She scoops up the ball but hesitates, slips one tackle and almost ducks into another. She might be slippery but she doesn't have enough awareness of where her support is. Ava's yelling, trying to direct her. Ava clears a path to allow Poppy to short kick to Grace on the wing. Grace doesn't waste time and takes off. She has 15 metres on her opponent. There's great shepherding by her teammate, Ruby.

Grace kicks along the boundary – looks like it's going over the line. But no! Elly, the ex-soccer fanatic, knocks it back in and then continues her run along the wing. There's nothing on offer up forward, but she's got space, so takes one bounce, two bounces. Zoe calls out for her to have a shot. Elly launches the ball from 30. The Ravens defenders go for the ball, missing it by centimetres. It bounces over their heads and goes through! What a goal! Might be one for the team highlights clip. The Scorpions are pumped! For the first time, they are leading the game.

Look at those girls gather round Elly. She must be pleased that she moved over to Aussie Rules now. Not long to go till half-time. Back in the centre, the Ravens are starting to show some nerves. Hit-out by Heidi who's clipped in the thigh by Rose's wandering leg in the ruck duel. She goes down but gets up quick enough to swat the footy into the open where the Ravens pounce. A kick across the body by a Ravens player lands in the hands of their half forward. She plays on quickly. Obviously speed is the plan to get the drop on the Scorpions. Oh, that's a perfect kick towards their goal. It's going to land 20 metres out. Whoa! Isabella takes off after a powerful intercept mark. Where did she come from?

The Scorpions' crowd goes wild. Soooo loud! That roar could be heard at the MCG. Isabella isn't waiting around, breaking the lines with support from Chandra who points to Emma further up the ground. There's a spearing pass to Emma who tracks back, wheels and sees Matilda, who has run the length of the field and is in open space running towards goal. She marks, bounces and goal! Another one for the Scorpions. And kicked by one of their backs. Gee, don't the backs love kicking a goal. Needless to say, Joe has gone berserk. His cheering sounds like a jet passing over. This has certainly set the cat amongst the pigeons. ***GO SCORPIONS!!***

That's back-to-back-to-back goals for the Scorpions. They're rushing over to Matilda and giving Isabella, Chandra and Emma slaps on the back for their part in that play. Magnificent movement of the ball. Both teams settle and move back into position. The siren goes for half-time just as the ball is bounced. But wait, where's Heidi? In all that excitement, nobody's noticed the champion ruck limping. In fact, she can hardly walk and slumps to the ground. Her dad, Andy, rushes over to see what's wrong. Anna is close on his heels with her medical kit.

Third Decision Point:

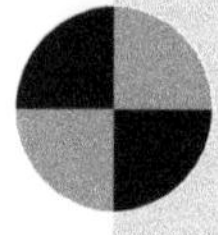

Is Heidi out for the rest of the game?

Go to page 72

OR

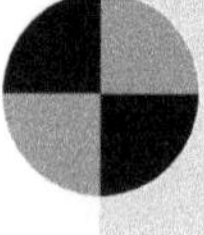

Does Heidi recover and return after half-time?

Go to page 82

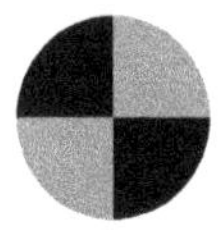

You decided that Talia misses an easy goal.

Zoe gives Talia some encouraging words and steps back. Talia has a long run-up and is usually deadly accurate, especially when she is on the run with no time to think about mistakes. The Scorpions really need this goal to help settle their nerves. Talia runs in, kicks and the ball goes straight, but at the last second it veers to the right and Talia misses the lot. Out of bounds on the full. The crowd groans. From 20 out it should've been a sure thing. Probably a combination of nerves and not accounting for the breeze that's blowing across the ground. Her teammates run by and tell her not to worry, but Talia looks pretty disappointed with herself. So the Scorpions are still left with that solitary point kicked by Zoe and still without their first goal.

Ravens waste no time in taking the free kick tight up against the point post. Their back pocket player waits for it, but hang on! Here comes Grace, who has slipped her tagger, and chops it off. Talia runs by, receives a slick handball from Grace and slots a goal! A beautiful goal! Obviously she kicks better when she doesn't have to think about it. You can overthink things in footy, as the coach often says. Teammates run to her from everywhere, celebrating their first goal in this game and their first in the competition. Zoe hugs Talia and, laughing, says, 'Way better than my point.'

That goal lifts the Scorpions' spirits and they find a new spring in their step.

There's not long to go before half-time and the Scorps want another goal while the Ravens want to get one back in a hurry. Nobody wins the ruck battle with all the mids throwing everything into the fight. Ravens win the battle on the ground and their on-baller, Maddy, streaks away. The move looks ominous for the Scorpions' defence as the Ravens have got plenty of players up forward. For sure the Ravens want to teach this new team a lesson. They want the Scorpions to feel the pain and to know their place. They are not happy that the Scorpions are up and about.

The Scorpions' backline manages to repel each Ravens attack that sends the ball deep into Ravens' territory. Hannah, Isabella, Beth and Holly are throwing everything into defence. Another deep entry from the Ravens but they seem to be just bombing it long. The Scorpions are really applying the pressure. The ball finally comes to ground and Matilda swats it. It goes some 30 metres and, as luck would have it, falls into Sophie's hands. She takes off and goes for a run. There's not much in front of her though. Ravens come at her and she almost slips over, but gets it out to Elly before the Ravens catch up. Jasmine, who's just come off the bench, is on her own in the 50-metre arc. She's screaming for the ball. They need to get it down to her. Elly probably can't kick that far.

Now Jasmine is picked up by Ravens' defence. Sophie hasn't stopped running forward, setting up options. Maybe here's a chance for Elly to get it to Sophie. But too late. Elly's tackled – she's waited too long to get rid of it. Free kick to the Ravens who try to rush a kick which is smothered by Elly and she gathers the loose ball. Sophie's only metres away.

Elly passes to her with a nice short kick. Sophie twists, turns and gets around two opponents. She knows the siren's about to sound so she decides to go for it with a long, long bomb from 50 metres out. It goes very deep. Ball bounces, bounces, no defence there. It's rolling. It's rolling. Siren for half-time sounds. Ball goes through the big sticks. But did it beat the siren?

Third Decision Point:

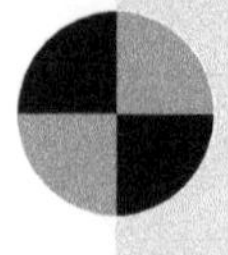

Does the ball beat the siren and go through for a goal?

Go to page 93

OR

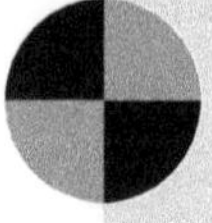

Does the ball go through after the siren sounds?

Go to page 106

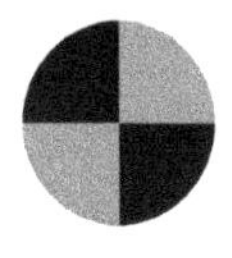

You decided that the coach chooses her daughter, the fast-running Ivy, to take Sophie's place in the centre.

The game is held up while Sophie is carried from the field and taken to hospital. The coach has a quick word to Ivy before she goes on. 'Focus! Tell the girls to focus on the game and I'll let them know about Sophie when we hear from her parents.'

The Scorpions will miss her agility and speed, but Ivy is also renowned for her acceleration and being able to run out a game. She's probably the right replacement for Sophie. Years of Little Athletics is a factor here as well. Brenda had to make a hard decision. She could've gone for the more experienced Bec, but at this stage the Scorps need pace and plenty of it because it seems to worry the Ravens.

The coach has called for quick ball movement. As Ivy runs to the centre, Scorpions and supporters give a cheer, so it doesn't seem as though the coach's decision has gone down badly. Talia has moved into the ruck and Heidi has moved forward to give some height to their forward line. Zoe yells, 'C'mon Scorps! Let's do it for Sophie.'

The game restarts with a throw-up. Ivy takes the tap from Talia and gets it out to Emma who loses it to Ravens mids who get it to their outside players. Confronted by Holly and Chandra, the Ravens player takes a chance and handballs high over the heads of the Scorpions' backs. A big group of players descend and there's a real tussle. It would be lucky if there's no ball-up. Ball spills out, only 30 metres out from the

Ravens' goal. Again, there's a lot of congestion, and the ball wobbles out. Somehow, the Ravens' forward pocket gets boot to ball and goal! It's a very lucky shot but nevertheless the Ravens get a goal. But they need more if they want some breathing space.

	GOALS	BEHINDS	TOTAL
WESTPARK SCORPIONS	2	0	12
EASTVALE RAVENS	2	1	13

Back in the centre, the players position themselves. Clearly all of the Scorps are worried about their teammate, Sophie. For many, it's the first time they have seen a teammate carried off and taken to hospital. The Scorpions mids exchange worried glances. 'Let's do it for Sophie!' yells Ivy. 'Let's do it for Sophie!' Ivy moves to the back of the ball-up, hoping to collect the footy. She's not a real strong girl so we don't expect to see her busting packs wide open. She relies mainly on her agility, speed and reading of the play.

The teams go at it with greater urgency in another ruck duel. Half-time's not far away and the Scorpions don't want the Ravens to get too far ahead. Ivy, playing a real smart midfielders' game, emerges with the ball and takes off but decides to handball it to Poppy. Bit of a 'hospital handpass' leaving Poppy without any time to move the ball along. Ravens corral Poppy and take her to the ground. She didn't get rid of the ball in time and it's a free kick to the Ravens. Ivy should have gone further with her run instead of handballing to Poppy. She knows she's fast. For just a millisecond she doubted herself and panicked. She should have more confidence in her run and carry.

Meanwhile, the Ravens kick further downfield but luckily for the Scorpions it's another turnover. Ava's got it and she kicks it back to her sister, Poppy. The Scorpions now have the ability to change direction. Poppy kicks across field to Ivy and it's the speedster again with a chance. This time she doesn't handball and backs her speed. Teammates scream at her to have a go. Clock's ticking and siren looming . . . Ivy sprints down the ground and evades one tackle, ducks the next, almost loses her footing. With half-time only seconds away, Ivy, unbalanced, regains her footing and kicks across her body. The ball sails through the air and it's a GOAL! Scorpions players run from everywhere to congratulate her. Ivy's speed and agility allowed her to outplay the Ravens' defence! Go Ivy and good decision Coach Brenda!

The siren sounds for half-time. The Scorpions are jubilant! The Ravens' breathing space evaporates.

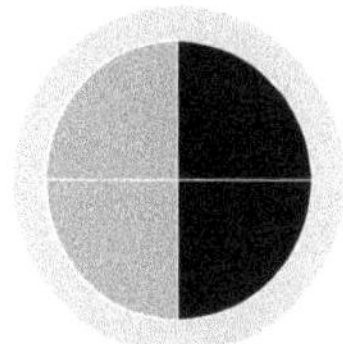

HALF-TIME

The Scorpions return to their change rooms. Coach Brenda doesn't waste time.

'C'mon girls. Get your drinks. Go to the toilet. Whatever you have to do, do it quickly. We have to make some decisions.' Some of the players look at their coach. They've not often seen her so charged up.

Most of the team are so excited to be ahead at this stage of the game. Too excited probably. Coach Brenda claps and Andy reminds them to get a move on, do what they have to do and stay focussed.

'All right girls!' yells Brenda. 'Listen to me please. Now I know you're worried about Sophie. I've just heard from Anna that she's doing okay and that she's being looked after.' The team applauds this welcoming news.

'Well, girls, that was a great quarter. Full of effort.'

'And what a goal by Ivy, Coach,' says Bec. Coach and Ivy appear embarrassed.

'Yes, yes good goal, Ivy.' Brenda allows herself a grin. The whole team, supporters and assistants laugh. They know Brenda doesn't want to be showing favouritism to her daughter, but like any mum, she couldn't help but feel proud. 'Okay. We've got a few decisions to make. I've been talking with Andy and Anna and Zoe. I'm thinking of making a few big changes for the second half. Changes that probably won't be liked too much. The Ravens are looking threatening, mainly due to their two talls up forward. Certainly Isabella, Chandra and our other backs have done a brilliant job so far. So no criticism there. But I'm thinking of switching Isabella and Talia. Isabella up forward and Talia down back. Hopefully it'll throw the Ravens off their game and Talia can stop their two talls. I know this is a big move.'

Most of the girls seem a bit unsure of this tactic, glancing at each other. But Talia and Isabella don't look too worried.

Third Decision Point:

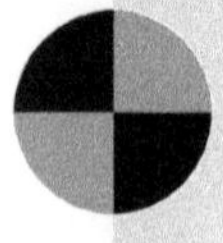

Does Coach make the switch?

Go to page  117

OR

Does Coach decide against making the switch?

Go to page  126

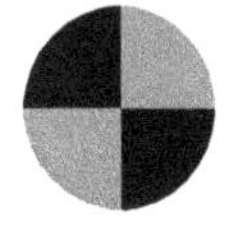

You decided that Coach chooses the very experienced Bec to take Sophie's place in the Centre.

The Scorpions were riding high, but Sophie's injury has taken the wind out of their sails. With Sophie on her way to hospital, Bec moves to the centre. Although she's feeling a little nervous about taking on this role, she's up for it nevertheless. She's not going to give up easily. She played in the mixed comp down the coast until she was 12, and for years she's kicked a footy in the backyard with her three older brothers, two of whom play for the Scorpions Boys. They're all here today to support Bec and the rest of the team. Bec has a quick chat with Zoe and Talia who's come back into the ruck to give Heidi a rest on the interchange. Talia is not as experienced as Heidi, but her height will worry the Ravens. There are only minutes to go till half-time.

The match restarts and both teams go at it. Neither team is backing off and there's a fierce struggle in the centre; a bit of pushing and shoving. The ball is somewhere under that pack. The umpire calls for the ball and throws it up. Another battle, but the umpire blows her whistle and pulls out a free, which goes to Bec. She decides to send it wide to Zoe who holds up play waiting for her Scorpions to arrive downfield. A beautiful long field kick into the forward arc, where the helmeted Emma rises, grabs, but can't control the ball to the ground. 'Play on' is the call and Ravens backs scoop it up and decide to go down the centre. A dangerous thing to do at any time, but the Ravens are free and creating impressive overlap running. Scorpions are clearly rattled by

Sophie's injury and despite trying to throw everything at them, the Ravens easily get the ball up to their full forward who finds herself all alone in the goal square. With lots of time, the Ravens' full forward calmly turns around and boots it through. Goal! Exactly what the Scorpions did not want to happen.

Back in the centre, it's a ball-up but the siren goes for half-time. Disappointed, the Scorpions walk off the ground in dribs and drabs while the Ravens sprint off in a group. Scorpions are only one point behind, however the goal on the half-time siren has sapped their confidence.

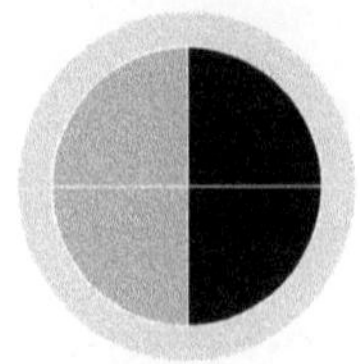

HALF-TIME

The change rooms are strangely quiet. The Scorpions are trying not to show signs of panic. Coach has a quick word with Bec who has been doing very well. She wants her to get in and under, and get the ball to the outside runners. Bec nods in agreement. Captain Zoe is wandering through the rooms checking on her teammates and giving them a bit of encouragement. The Scorpions were going well until that last goal by the Ravens knocked them around a bit.

Brenda gathers the girls together. 'Okay, girls. Just want you all to know that Sophie is okay and is recovering. Now that should lift our spirits. Come on, girls. Nobody said this was going to be an easy game. They're a very experienced

team and they're not going to give up their advantage without a fight. They especially don't want to be beaten by us. We can use that. No dropped heads. Come out firing. Who knows, the Ravens just might get the fumbles if we keep up the pressure. I want you to keep going the way you've been playing. Head over the ball. Look for your opportunities. And remember we're a team. Not a bunch of individuals kicking a footy around. All right, all hands in!'

The team bunches together and yells, ***'SCORPIONS!!'***

THIRD QUARTER

Centre bounce and Bec has certainly followed Coach's advice. I don't know what she learned in the backyard playing with her brothers but look out! Talk about an in-and-under player who's never frightened to go in for the hard ball. Ball comes down to no one in particular and there's a scramble in the middle. Bec is in the midst of it all at the bottom of the pack. Eventually, she gets the ball but is tackled high. A Ravens player nearly took her head off. Free to Bec and she immediately passes out wide to Thao who's moved up the ground. With space, Thao handballs to a player running past; looks like Jasmine. She bombs it long into the forward line, but Ravens' defence is disciplined and mark the ball. Heidi intercepts the kick and marks. A long kick by Heidi sees the ball coming back for the second time. Scorps have to take advantage of these forward entries otherwise the Ravens will make them pay. They'll use these entries and turn them into their advantage.

Ruby marks and immediately kicks high and the ball spins through the air. A Ravens full back punches it 20 metres – huge punch! Ravens descend on the footy like there's no tomorrow. They want to turn this game around. A Scorpions player goes in with tremendous courage. It's the smallest girl in the team, Poppy. There's a push in the back. She wastes no time with the free kick. She lowers her eyes and finds Bec 20 metres out on an angle. She doesn't waste time either and with a wonderful checkside kick, it goes through for a goal! Nice that Bec got that goal, considering her work rate so far.

Scorpions run from all over and high-five Bec, big smiles on their faces. Relieved and happy, Bec runs back to the centre.

Now that the Scorpions have got their tails up, the Ravens look rattled. At the centre bounce, Heidi gets the tap and the Scorpions attack like they know they're good enough. Bec knocks it onto Emma, and she short passes to Ivy 40 metres out from the Scorpions' goal. Scorpions forwards are making leads all over the place, but checked by Ravens' defence. Ivy adjusts her socks and lines up for a shot at goal. This one is a crucial kick. This would put the Scorpions up by almost two goals. It's a long kick for anyone. She doesn't know whether she's got the legs. Hang on! By the way she's holding the ball, she might be going for the big torpedo, the big barrel!

Third Decision Point:

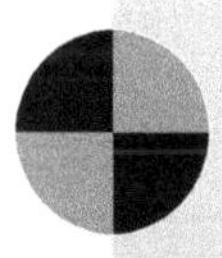

Does Ivy decide to kick a torpedo?

Go to page 135

OR

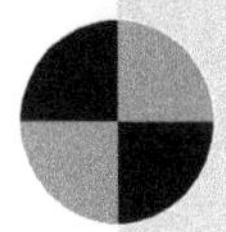

Does Ivy decide against kicking a torpedo?

Go to page 145

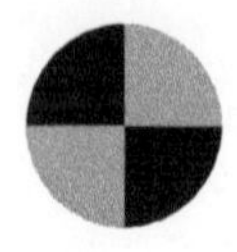

You decided that Heidi was out for the rest of the game.

Heidi sits on the bench with what looks like ten ice packs on that leg. Soon after the half-time siren sounded, she was carried from the ground. From the pain on her face, there is no way she'll return to the game. Anna is still tending to her. Andy hovers but Heidi shoos him away.

Coach Brenda congratulates the girls on a very fine team effort but she faces the big problem of deciding what to do about her ruck. She has a few choices: Isabella is tall and tough enough; Talia is definitely tall enough; or maybe even Emma who played defence in her basketball days. Coach chats with Zoe and Andy, and finally decides on Emma. A big call that one. Emma has had little experience rucking and it will deplete their on-ball brigade, but Jasmine will move into the Centre to cover that. That's a good choice – she's a good reader of the play. These moves will test Brenda's coaching experience.

Before they move out, Coach Brenda says, 'Made a few moves but they shouldn't confuse you. Stick to your own roles and keep doing what you're doing. All right, all hands in!'

The team bunches together and yells, ***'SCORPIONS!!'***

THIRD QUARTER

Off we go for the second half and things are becoming very intense. Not that the Ravens think they've got it in the bag, but they probably think a win is more likely with Heidi no longer in the game. The umpire has warned Rose, the Ravens ruck, about that wayward leg. The ball goes up and Emma out-bodies her opponent. Down into a scrimmage and the umpire says, 'Give it to me.' Again, Emma is using her muscle but this time to little effect. The Ravens take it away.

There's a good tackle in the Ravens' forward half by Elly who finds the ball and slips a pass to Poppy. Unfortunately Thao gets in her way and Poppy loses the ball in a Ravens' tackle. A free kick to the Ravens who don't waste time. A quick

handball to a teammate who kicks from an impossible angle – not effective at all. The Scorpions' defence goes into hyperdrive. Isabella, in her eagerness, clashes with her teammate, Hannah, allowing Ravens a quick kick out of the pack. Luckily for the Scorpions, it's only a behind. Zoe urges her players to keep up their concentration. A few silly mistakes could cost them on the scoreboard and really undo all their good work to date.

Friendly fire continues to be a problem. The Scorpions' backline is being made to work hard. Isabella looks for options. She goes one way, then the other and suddenly she's off, kicking down the line. Scorps are lining up for this ball. Ruby takes a nice safe mark but hurries her kick and it goes out of bounds on the full. Ravens' kick-in. There's a fantastic intercept mark by Chandra who is clearly sick of mucking around. She sees Grace in the middle, who collects the ball at ground level. There's growing confidence as she heads towards the Scorps' goal and does a look-away handball to Emma, the Scorps' new ruck, who runs around her opposite number and drills a goal. That should place a big tick next to Coach's decision on Emma.

Siren sounds for the end of the quarter.

	GOALS	BEHINDS	TOTAL
WESTPARK SCORPIONS	4	1	25
EASTVALE RAVENS	2	1	13

The only thing that Brenda wants to emphasise at three-quarter time is for the Scorpions not to get too over-confident. Heidi has joined them in the huddle. Although she's all taped up, she assures everyone that she's all right. Brenda doesn't make any changes but says, 'Make sure you keep the talk going on out there. That'll help avoid some of the friendly fire that's happening.'

Andy chimes in, 'And good effort Emma!' Some join in with pats on the back, others wolf down oranges and gulp water. The team is certainly feeling the tiredness in their legs and realise that they're now in the big-time.

The team huddles together and yells, ***'GO SCORPIONS!!'***

FINAL QUARTER

The final quarter begins and there's a wild kick by some player – it's hard to see who. It goes out towards the wing and lands in the hands of a Ravens player. With an open field in front of her, she has no one to kick it to. She passes sideways. Ravens are being patient, playing a possession game – showing their experience here. They're not panicking, realising they can't lose their heads if they want to have any chance of getting back in the lead. Now Ravens kick backwards. Some people don't like this tactic but it allows teams to keep possession until something emerges downfield. Scorpions are looking nervous; they're unsure how to keep the Ravens in check. They know the Ravens can take off if they're allowed to. The Ravens have players loose all over the ground. The siren may not be too far away and the Scorpions might be well ahead, but they are right to worry about the Ravens' ability to bounce back. Here comes Kaitlyn, the Ravens' forward, who goes to the Ravens' pocket. Holly chops off Kaitlyn's poor kick. As though she hears her coach's words echoing in her ears, she evades a tackle and goes long to the wing.

Another turnover by the Scorpions and the Ravens mount yet another attack. The ball goes over the back of the pack and Isabella snares it. She had the option of a rushed behind but she has the confidence to keep it in play and does a sweeping handball to Matilda in the back pocket who in turn kicks to Grace, who teams up with Zoe. And now they run it through the lines. Ruby comes on board and the three of them work together. They've really opened up this passage of play, sowing confusion in the Ravens' defence. Ruby handballs back to Zoe. A beautiful foot pass finds Thao who loves to run and bounce. Once, twice, shrugs off a tackler, 30 metres out, kicks off the outside of her boot and GOAL. Sensational goal! Siren sounds!! Outside of the boot isn't a simple kick but Thao executed it beautifully.

The Westpark Scorpions Under 14 Girls have won their very first game. They rush to each other; hugging and jumping and high-fiving. It's a bit like a Grand Final victory. Poppy and Ava are overwhelmed with tears of joy. Captain Zoe runs to the boundary to give her mum and dad a high-five. Heidi limps onto the ground and the Scorpions run to her. A comprehensive first win AND against one of the best teams in the Under 14 Girls competition.

GO SCORPIONS!!

WIN

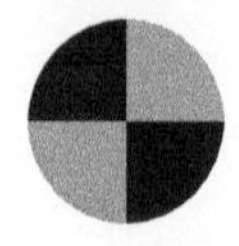

You decided that Heidi recovers and returns after half-time.

Anna helps Heidi off the field and immediately gets to work on that leg of hers. Looks like a very bad bruise; you can see it going black and blue. She copped a bad knock from Rose's outstretched boot. Umpires need to warn Rose about this action. Meanwhile, Coach is chatting to Zoe and Andy about Heidi. At this stage, they're not sure what changes they might have to make.

The third quarter is about to start and Heidi is recovering on the bench with medico Anna by her side. Coach Brenda calls on Talia to take over the ruck work. She moves Emma to full forward, mainly due to her experience playing in various positions, and Ivy takes on the follower's role.

'You've done so well girls. Some of you might have only dreamed of this but here we are in the lead.' A rousing cheer goes up. 'But let's face it, the Ravens are not done yet so let's keep up the good work. And there's no reason why we shouldn't stay in front! All right, all hands in!'

The team bunches together and yells, ***'SCORPIONS!!'***

THIRD QUARTER

With the Scorps up by seven points, they have been warned by Coach Brenda not to ease up the pressure. Take their foot off the pedal and the Ravens will leave them in their wake. They've obviously received a rocket from their coach. The Ravens' on-ballers work overtime. Sophie takes it away, but is brought to ground. It's a free to the Ravens and now there's been a switch on. A good kick out wide is picked up by Kaitlyn, the Ravens' forward, who bangs it quickly ahead of her but nobody can take it cleanly. Lots of players want that footy. The ball is brought to ground. There are bodies falling everywhere. Hannah gets a handball out to Beth who loses possession. Is that a free? No, the umpire doesn't think so. A Raven gets it out and somehow short kicks it to her teammate standing all alone 20 metres out. Another short pass goes to a Ravens teammate, directly in front. She goes back and calmly puts it through the hey diddle diddle. Ravens high-five each other and now it's looking dangerous for the Scorpions. It's a one-point difference.

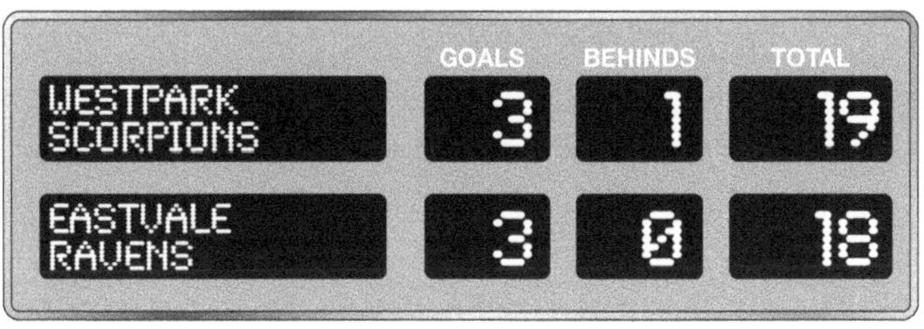

The game goes on with neither side giving an inch. This is sometimes called the 'Championship Quarter', with every player giving their all. And now what do we see? Heidi doing warm-ups and short sprints along the boundary line without an obvious limp. Anna and her famous liniment oil seem to have done the trick. Not to mention her massaging ability. Runner Andy has been given the message and now Heidi comes back onto the ground. Talia returns to full forward and Heidi is back in the ruck. Things return to normal, which is hectic to say the least. There's still only one point separating the two teams.

Now the ball is knocked out of bounds. Rucks and on-ballers position themselves for the throw-in. Heidi jostles with Rose, who keeps that leg of hers down, and wins the contest to the cheers of the Scorpions. Joe waves his BBQ tongs in the air like spears. The ball comes to Elly who executes a quick kick, but oh no! She didn't see the Ravens' opposition who smothers the ball and then picks it up. She quickly executes a precise field kick under pressure to Ravens' forward Kaitlyn, who comes in and takes the mark while running with the flight of the ball. No Scorpion is on the mark. The ball is moved too quickly by the Ravens so she turns and puts it through the big sticks. The Ravens are making the Scorpions pay for Elly's mistake. This is certainly different from training drills.

At three-quarter time, Coach Brenda points out some mistakes being made: going too slow; not lowering their eyes when going forward; and not standing on the mark. She decides against making any changes and asks the girls to offer up an honest, never-give-up response. The last quarter is coming up.

FINAL QUARTER

The final quarter begins and the crowd's on its feet, sensing that the game's coming down to the wire. Even with Heidi back on field, the Scorpions don't seem to have the same passion they were playing with earlier in the game. Or maybe it's just exhaustion and not being used to the pressure that comes with this level of competition. Playing comp games takes so much more energy, not to mention all the excitement and hype that goes with it. Let's hope the girls have the legs to finish off the game.

The Scorpions seem to be giving their utmost. Heidi wins the ruck duel immediately. Her injury certainly hasn't stopped her great ruck work, but the tap goes straight to a Ravens player, roving well. Sophie launches into a tackle and wins a free for incorrect disposal. And she's off, arching her back. Sophie seems to be taking on the game all by herself. She's got teammates screaming for the ball but she ignores all of them, gets to 40 metres and goes for it. Going. Going. At the last second it veers away to the right and it's only a behind for the Scorpions. Which is not what they need at this stage of the game with the seconds ticking away.

Only four points in it and the crowd is going crazy. A chant started up by Joe and Anna gains momentum. Lizzie, Isabella's grandmother, waves her hands in the air. Coach tells Andy to tell the girls not to flood backwards, as it will leave them nothing up forward to get that all important goal.

Ravens kick it out. Someone marks in the pocket, then kicks to her on-baller who is loose in the centre of the ground. Dangerous kick. Had to be perfect and it was. Ravens are taking their time, trying to take some seconds off the clock. Siren can't be too far away now. She kicks it wide. Ball bounces but a Ravens teammate collects it and, looking for a target, she goes for Kaitlyn, who marks it on her chest. She does a short kick on to Maddy who is running past. She dodges the desperate tackles from Beth who is showing signs of panic. Maddy delivers it to Ravens' ruck, Rose, who has drifted forward. A nice, clean mark. She's looking for some leads; the options up front are all closely checked by Scorpions.

There is no clear avenue to the Ravens' goal. Great defensive work by the Scorpions, but they might possibly run out of time to snatch a win. The siren is due at any second and the Scorpions are desperate to turn this game around. Rose is still looking for forward options.

Siren goes!! The Ravens' crowd goes wild. Rose brings home another goal before celebrating with her teammates. Which she does amidst the cheers from the Ravens.

The Scorpions' crowd is in tears. It's the first loss for the Scorpions, but a valiant effort nonetheless. The Scorpions were ahead for a considerable time, making this loss a bitter pill to swallow. The Scorpion girls come together and trudge off the ground as one. It was the right decision for Heidi to play out the game. Brenda gathers the team together, telling them to lose well is equally important as celebrating a win. A ten-point loss against last year's Premiers is not too bad, especially given it was their first real match in the competition. The team huddles together and as one shout, ***'SCORPIONS!!'***

	GOALS	BEHINDS	TOTAL
WESTPARK SCORPIONS	3	2	20
EASTVALE RAVENS	5	0	30

LOSS

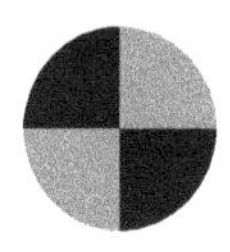

You decided that the ball beat the siren and went through for a goal.

Absolute elation explodes amongst the Scorpions as the umpire signals the all-clear. The honking sounds like twenty car alarms going off at the same time. A goal for the Scorpions on the siren at half-time sees them in front. Not a bad first half of competition football for the newest team.

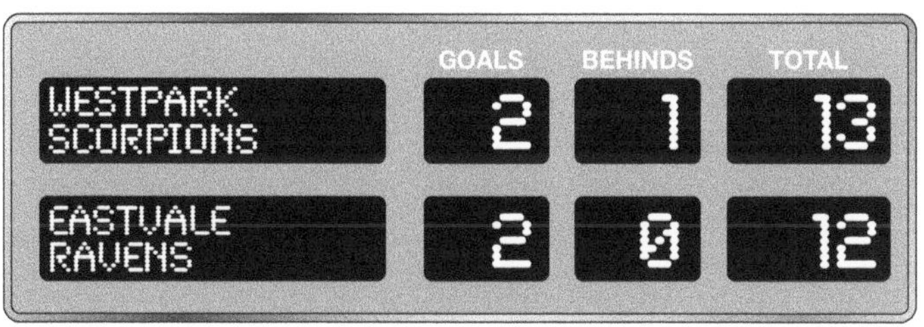

	GOALS	BEHINDS	TOTAL
WESTPARK SCORPIONS	2	1	13
EASTVALE RAVENS	2	0	12

Coach congratulates the team on their never-say-die attitude. Coach Brenda wants more of the same. 'The Ravens are going to be livid about that last goal, so watch out. They'll come out all guns firing. They do NOT want to be beaten by us,' she says. 'Okay, if you need to get taped up or need liniment into your muscles, get it done. Oranges are on the bench and don't drop the peel on the ground. Good work Scorpions. All right, all hands in!'

The team bunches together and yells, ***'SCORPIONS!!'***

THIRD QUARTER

The Scorps run out onto the ground. They have smiles on their faces and a spring in their step. We'll see how this translates onto the field. Players get in position. Ravens continue with their pushing and shoving. They've obviously been told to put more heat on this new unseasoned team by intimidating them with these tactics, which they've done since the start of the game. Beth and Thao seem to be copping the worst but they're not the type to take that kind of physical action lying down. Beth gives one good push back to her opposite number and that Ravens player falls to the ground. Andy, who's out there giving last minute instructions, sees it but then heads towards the bench, pretending not to.

Ball-up and the third quarter begins.

The pushing and roughhousing continues. The umpire tells the girls to tone it down. She doesn't want the game to get out of control. For an Under 14 game, it is unusual to see. Heidi goes for a big hit-out and it sails towards the Scorpions' goals. The Ravens' backs run faster and are first to pick up the ball as it rolls towards the Scorpions' goal. The Ravens collect the ball and run through the corridor. It's a dangerous tactic, going straight up the middle; one mistake and your opponents will seize their chance and take the ball from your possession. Which is exactly what happens. The Ravens player takes one too many bounces, and with Ava snapping at her heels, she gets off a hurried kick which lands in space where Sophie gathers and sends it back with a high and long kick to Scorpions forwards. Talia brings it down to ground where Zoe, who is front and centre, snares the ball and evades a tackle. She's looking to give it off, but there's nothing on offer. She wheels away from the goals, turns and kicks with her left foot. Through the big sticks it goes. What a Captain's goal!! Now this will really set the cat amongst the pigeons.

In the centre, Andy gives messages from the coach. It looks like Isabella is going to give Heidi a rest. Isabella is now in the ruck and Heidi is down to full back. Interesting move. Ravens have been stung by that last goal. They see it as a real challenge to their status as the more experienced team. All over the ground the

Ravens are becoming even more physical, which is a nice way of saying they're pushing, shoving and hanging on. Isabella doesn't give an inch. The ball goes up and she wins the tap out, but Ravens on-baller, Maddy, steals the footy and boots it out to the wing where Ravens take it long down the line. Hannah gets into a tussle with a Ravens forward and nearly has her head taken off, but no free kick. Don't know how the umpire missed that one and neither does the crowd.

'What about a free, umpy?' someone yells. Hannah remembers Coach Brenda's advice that the umpire is always right!

There's a high kick into the Ravens' forward line. A pack gathers. Heidi flies and takes a stupendous mark in defence. Seems that the Isabella-Heidi move has paid off. Heidi takes her time with the ball. Looks like she copped a whack from a Ravens player – she's holding her side and grimacing in pain. The umpire tells her to play on. Holly runs past and takes a handball from Heidi. Holly gets it off to Chandra who switches play. Looks like a promising idea, but the siren goes for three-quarter time. Immediately, Andy is out there telling Heidi to have herself checked out by Anna and instructing the other girls to get into the huddle as quickly as possible.

There's a sense of urgency in Coach Brenda's voice. 'Excellent ruck work Isabella and one of the best marks of the day from Heidi. By the way, are you okay after that hit? Do you need to stay off?' Heidi shakes her head and says she's fine. Brenda continues. 'We made those changes to keep the Ravens guessing and show them we have players who can perform in any position. It seems to have unsettled them judging by the amount of shoving going on. Don't get sucked into their nonsense, but don't take it lying down either. They'll come unstuck if they keep doing it. Heidi, you go back into the ruck and Isabella head down back. Sophie have a rest. Jasmine into the Centre. All right, all hands in!'

The team bunches together and yells, ***'SCORPIONS!!'***

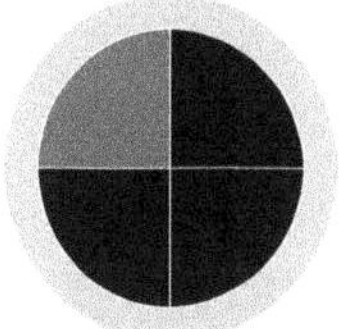

FINAL QUARTER

The fourth and final quarter is underway. The Ravens' pushing and scragging continues. The umpire warns that she'll start giving 25-metre penalties if the bad behaviour continues. Emma retaliates and dumps a Ravens player. Whistle blows and it's a free to the Ravens. The Ravens player has a big smile on her face while Emma looks annoyed with herself. Ravens go for the big bomb to half forward and there's a strong pack mark to the forward, Kaitlyn. Cheers go up from Ravens' supporters. Kaitlyn goes back. She's dead in front and 30 metres out. Comes in and sprays the kick wide. It sneaks in for a behind.

Meanwhile, Andy is out there talking to Emma, telling her to keep a cool head. Scorpions will have to take things in their stride and take on Brenda's advice. Hannah kicks out with a neat kick to the pocket. Matilda runs around her opposite number, getting it to Jasmine who holds up the flow. She's playing a possession game. Jasmine kicks sideways to Zoe who is corralled and tackled but doesn't lose the ball. Zoe's surrounded by about ten players. It's a very scrappy affair with bodies lunging desperately. A pack forms and Zoe is dragged over the line still in possession. Lucky not to have a free paid against her.

Throw-in. Another scrap, and the ball

squirts out the back. Grace bends to pick it up. She's tackled before she has a chance, but tackled when not in possession and dumped on the ground. That's a free kick to Grace. The umpire has lost patience and gives a 25-metre penalty. Grace gets on with it – no time for calm thinking now. Downfield, there is nothing much on offer. The ball reaches another messy pack where Ravens fight hard. The footy rolls out and Thao sees her chance. With Ravens defenders hot on her tail, trying to tackle her, Thao runs off, and slips over while bouncing the ball. She still has the ball under her control. Teammates call for a handpass and Thao manages to knock the ball onto Emma in the goal square. Wow, Emma appeared out of nowhere!

Emma's got it now, but slips over. Cool as a cucumber, she manages to somehow get her foot to the ball while she's on the ground and through the big sticks it goes. Ravens look stunned. How did they let that one through?! Well, it doesn't matter now – there's the siren for the end of the game.

Parents rush onto the ground, hugging and kissing their daughters. The Scorpions gather around Emma, celebrating her amazing goal. There are celebrations all around. Loads of clapping and cheering from all the Scorpions' supporters. Joe throws more sausages on the BBQ as the Scorpions jog off the ground together. A first team win for the Scorpions Under 14 Girls. Looks like the Scorpions have well and truly arrived!

GOALS
BEHINDS
TOTAL
WESTPARK SCORPIONS
4
1
25
EASTVALE RAVENS
2
1
13

WIN

THE
END

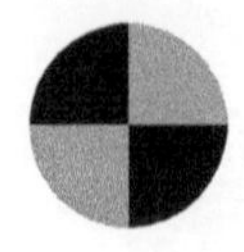

You decided that the ball went through after the siren sounds.

Coach Brenda speaks to the team as soon as they enter the change rooms at half-time, telling them not to worry about missing out on that goal. 'It was only a matter of milliseconds girls and we're still in the game – less than a goal behind. The ball rolled through just after the siren sounded. The main thing to take out of that passage of play is how we went about it, not forgetting efforts by Elly and Sophie. So the last thing we want to do is to keep on worrying about a goal we missed out on. Okay, get some fruit and drinks into you, have a bit of a rest and let's go get those Ravens. All right, all hands in!'

The team bunches together and yells, ***'SCORPIONS!!'***

THIRD QUARTER

By the time they run from the rooms, the sky is darkening with thunderclouds. All of the girls immediately look at Hannah who is grinning like a fish. Well-known for her love of playing in the mud and rain, she is ready for anything. Whether this suits the rest of the team, we're about to find out. Andy reminds the girls that if the rain really starts pouring they can forget about high marks and start thinking about how to move the ball forward.

'No kicking off the ground,' he reminds them.

Up goes the footy and both sides descend in a scramble. The rain is getting heavier. Hannah moves around as the ball comes down into the Ravens' half.

Looks like she's almost willing the ball her way. Rose, the Ravens' ruck, gets boot to ball and kicks it a long way into their forward zone. Footy spills out from the pack and rolls towards the Scorpions' back pocket. The Ravens appear desperate; they don't want it out of their forward 50. The ball continues to roll, almost over the boundary. The Ravens would be happy with that. Desperation from all sides. The Ravens have a chance for a goal. The Scorpions are trying to stop it. It's pretty ugly football at the moment. Nobody can keep their feet. The umpire calls for the ball and it's thrown up. Scorpions knock it out of the danger zone, but still nothing decisive. There's an absolute jumble of mud and players out there and the umpire calls for the ball yet again. She's trying to open up the game but the weather isn't helping.

Ball-up and Rose gets a neat tap and,

again, nothing comes of it. It seems like half the players from both sides are there in this torrential rain. A pack forms and Chandra somehow gets her hands on the footy and boots it away from danger. It lands on the ground with nobody near the ball, but once more we see the Ravens attacking. It's now covered in mud and is almost impossible to pick up.

The ball hasn't been out of the Ravens' forward line for ages. Now it's more of a struggle for the players to just stay on their feet. The ball slithers towards the boundary line, but Hannah, the mud and rain lover, manages to keep it in. Not sure whether that's a good idea in these conditions but Hannah uses the narrow space she's got to try and get a handball to Holly. The Ravens' forwards intercept Hannah's handball a short kick away from goal. The Ravens player knows what she's doing because her teammate,

Kaitlyn, is close by. Matilda's attempting to slow the Ravens down. She's going to have to be careful with her tackling which is almost too high. Ravens dodge grasping hands and somehow get boot to a sodden ball. It goes through for a goal as the siren sounds and Ravens run from all over the ground to congratulate their goal-kicker, Kaitlyn. They know how important that goal is with the weather becoming worse. The Scorpions are really up against it now in these conditions. Almost two goals down and only a quarter left to play.

FINAL QUARTER

Now the skies have really opened up and Coach Brenda has exhorted her team to get the ball forward no matter what. Isabella will go into the ruck to give Heidi a rest down back, although the backline might miss Isabella's grit. Then again, Hannah and Beth aren't too shabby either.

It's a wet and wild afternoon. The rain is pouring down and the raindrops seem as big as golf balls. It's difficult to see more than a few metres in front of you in this heavy downpour. Hopefully there won't be a thunderstorm which could stop the game. Ravens are now playing with belief and the game is looking more like rugby than Aussie Rules. Another big kick from a Ravens follower cuts deep into their forward line, almost to their goals. This will go close. A pack forms and over the top flies Hannah with a great punch through for a Ravens behind. She saved a sure goal and look at her – mud from top to toe but still has that grin from ear to ear. That took absolute courage.

	GOALS	BEHINDS	TOTAL
WESTPARK SCORPIONS	1	1	7
EASTVALE RAVENS	3	1	19

Isabella kicks long out of the backline, straight down the middle. Risky move, especially in this kind of weather. One mistake and that footy will be coming back into the Ravens' forward line faster than you can blink. Grace seizes the opportunity, keeping in mind that the smallest error will be something she might have nightmares about. She's finding it hard to keep on her feet now with the ground being so wet and slippery. She kicks – a small trip but it manages to reach the tallest girl on the field, Talia. Believe it or not, Talia bounces the ball in these conditions. A long handball to Elly who, for some reason, is all alone in front of goal. Elly bangs the sodden footy through the goals and the Scorpions haven't given up yet. With only a goal now separating the two teams, the Scorpions feel like they still have a chance in this game.

	GOALS	BEHINDS	TOTAL
WESTPARK SCORPIONS	2	1	13
EASTVALE RAVENS	3	1	19

Ball-up in the centre. Time is running out. There's a bit of panic on both sides now. Ravens are hanging onto their lead and Scorpions are desperate to wrest it from them. There are so many players milling around. Ball going nowhere, bodies toppling over, until Matilda manages to pick it up and handball to Ruby. Ravens players are in hot pursuit. Looks like we're heading for another throw-in but Ruby swipes at the footy, knocking it towards Elly who has found an extra pair of legs. She's about to pick it up when she gets a big, big bump from Ravens' defence. It sends Elly sprawling, allowing the Ravens player to gather and drive it forward, where it's marked by a Ravens follower a long way out from their goal. Great mark in these conditions where it's difficult to see more than a few metres in front of you. Ravens follower runs a few steps and bombs it towards goal, with a hope and a prayer and with the help of a sudden gust of wind, it goes through for a goal! A heartbreaker for the Scorpions.

Nobody can believe it. Neither the Scorpions nor the Ravens. What a kick and what a freakish gust of wind! Siren goes and game ends in these amazing circumstances. After a fiercely contested game, the Ravens come away with a strong win. The Scorpion girls are really saddened by a two-goal loss. They were still in the game with minutes to go.

Wet, drenched and covered in mud, the Scorpions slowly walk off the ground, still amazed by that last freakish goal by the Ravens. Welcome to the competition, Scorpions! A lesson learnt in their first match in football – the game's not over till it's over.

LOSS

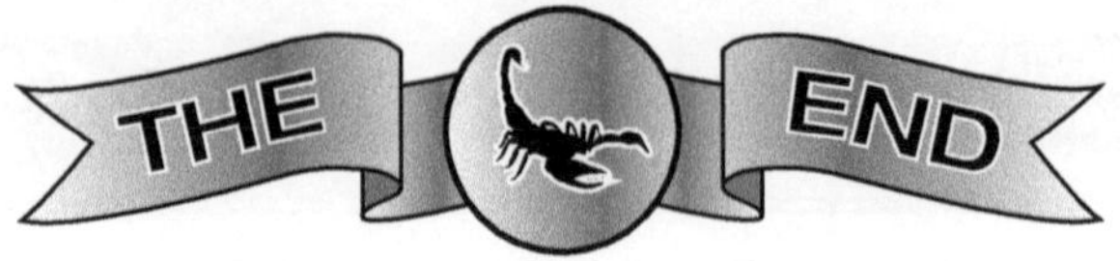

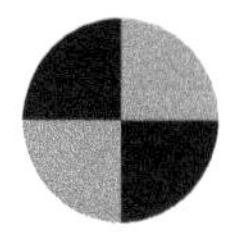

You decided that the coach makes the switch.

It is an interesting switch to make considering that it's the Scorps' first game in the comp. However, we'll wait and see. Brenda is no easy beat. She's been developing this team for a while now. The Scorpions were going well, almost level-pegging, but she must be thinking ahead and sees possible problems if she left things as they were. Isabella and Talia certainly seem to be taking things in their stride. It's common these days for players to be able to play in several positions. And by the look of the smile on Isabella's face, as a full back, she'll love the chance to kick goals.

THIRD QUARTER

And now we're away in this fascinating match. Heidi runs down to Emma, but the ball can't escape the pack with players from both sides struggling to get clean hands on the footy. And it's a ball-up again. Into the air it goes, but no real winner there. Ravens break clear via Maddy. Her smooth movement gets the ball down to their forward zone with a beautiful kick to Kaitlyn, who's making a perfect lead. They didn't count on Talia who leaps over the other players and punches it away to the boundary where it goes over the line.

Ravens are calling for the umpire to see it as deliberate, but nothing doing. Throw-in and again the Ravens attack, kicking for goal but it sails through for a behind. Not much thought went into that kick.

Scorpions give a cheer as Talia kicks out. Good to see a forward being able to take on the important task of kicking out. We're not sure whether this is in the playbook, but she's gone straight up the middle. Big competition for the ball here and a clash results in the ball getting into Jasmine's hands. She takes off like a rocket. Her handball over the top nearly comes unstuck, but Thao collects and sees Isabella streaming out from goal. A perfect pass. The ball clunks into Isabella's hands and big cheers go up from supporters. There should be no problem to score from only 20 metres out.

Isabella comes in and kicks but, oh no, it slides off the side of her boot for only one point. Nevertheless, the Scorpions are still five points in front. The siren sounds for the end of the third quarter. The final quarter is coming up and we'll see if the coach sticks to her guns concerning this switch.

There's a sense of excitement in Coach Brenda's voice. 'Great work rate girls and we are definitely in the game with a great chance of winning. Excellent defensive work Talia and great running Jasmine. Isabella, don't think about your last shot at goal, it will happen. We made those changes to keep the Ravens on their toes. If we continue to work hard as a team and play our game, we can win this!

Don't lose your heads. Keep thinking, focus and concentrate right through to the final siren. All right, all hands in!'

The team bunches together and yells, ***'SCORPIONS!!'***

FINAL QUARTER

The final quarter is about to get underway. Andy is out there talking to Isabella, probably telling her not to worry about that last kick. Yep, it's Isabella up forward and Talia full back. The switch is still on.

Play gets underway. Emma and Ivy are working hard, trying to make sure the ball doesn't fall into the wrong hands. Best intentions sometimes don't work out though as Emma pulls the ball under her and it's a free to the Ravens' on-baller, Maddy. The Ravens are racking up frees in this game. A Ravens player calls for it but is under enormous pressure when it arrives. She's tackled and the ball spills, but no free kick. The footy is now in the hands of Zoe, who's trying to increase her impact on this game. She's desperate to get it out and onwards. Zoe keeps running, paddles the ball in front of her. She picks it up but Ravens descend on her and it's lost almost immediately. Scorps are less than a goal in front but there's a bit of panic on both sides. The team who can keep their head will come out on top today.

Near the boundary line, about twelve players are in a very scrappy affair. The ball squirts out the back. Ruby is tackled when she bends to pick it up. But tackled when not in possession, so it's a free kick to Ruby. Ruby gets on with it, no time for slow thinking here. Downfield, there's nothing much on offer but she goes for it anyway. As the footy sails through the air, Isabella, the stand-in full forward, sees her chance. Nice mark. She plays on with Ravens defenders hot on her tail. The ball is still in her possession. Then, cool as a cucumber, Isabella kicks the ball across her body and through the big sticks it goes. Not too bad for a regular full back. Tough battle that one. There's the siren. The Scorpions win their first game by just 11 points!!

Pandemonium erupts. Kids run onto the ground. Isabella's mum wheels Lizzie onto the field. Lizzie cries tears of joy as Isabella gives her the biggest hug. Scorpions run from all over the ground to hug each other. Ravens players shake hands with the Scorpions and congratulate them on their first win. Good job! Hugs, laughter and high-fives. Zoe is beaming after her first win as Captain. Scorpions can't believe they have won their first game in the comp and against last year's Premiers too. Amazing! And with that brave switch, it looks like we have a new super coach in the comp. With a spring in their step, the girls jog off the ground into the change rooms and Joe leads the loudest three cheers from all the Scorpions' parents and supporters. ***GO SCORPIONS!!***

	GOALS	BEHINDS	TOTAL
WESTPARK SCORPIONS	4	1	25
EASTVALE RAVENS	2	2	14

WIN

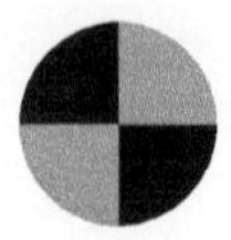

You decided that the coach doesn't make the switch.

At the last minute, Coach Brenda decides against the move, mainly because neither Isabella nor Talia have had much experience playing at opposite ends of the ground. Talia is secretly relieved while Isabella seems disappointed. Like most backs, she's probably had dreams of kicking at least one goal if not a bag of them.

Since Sophie was injured, Ivy has taken up the Centre position and there's no reason why that should change.

THIRD QUARTER

Away we go in this most interesting match. Some thought that the Scorpions were going to be swamped, but that's not the case as once again we see Ivy swoop on the ball and is away with her rockets on. A long low pass to Talia comes unstuck as the Ravens double-team her, punching the ball some 30 metres away in fact. Ball comes back into Ivy's hands and she decides to knock the ball onto Matilda further up the ground. A pack of Ravens attack and bring her to ground but the umpire calls, 'In the back.'

Matilda gets to her feet, looking a bit worse for wear. She kicks backwards to Talia who then takes it further back to Chandra. Scorpions will have to be careful here – the ball is deep in Ravens' territory. One slip up and the Ravens will score an easy goal. Chandra does a short pass to Isabella, an ever-reliable back who spies Emma in the middle, and it's a quick kick to her. Emma doubles back then boots it to Heidi who plucks the ball in a stunning pack mark. Heidi isn't sure what to do. Indecisive at first, she feints a handpass but kicks back to Emma instead. The Scorpions haven't moved forward much and remain on the wing. They can't afford to muck around here. Going backwards and forwards can only work for a short time.

Possession game here by the Scorpions. The umpire tells them to play on. Emma looks undecided. She will have to be quick. She finally makes a low foot pass up forward to Elly, whose ankle seems to be holding up. She finds space, chip passes to Talia who's not waiting around anymore. Talia takes on the

Ravens player standing on her mark, 40 metres out from the Scorpions' goal, and takes off. Oh, she's taken high!! Got her head ripped off. Although unintended by the Ravens player, it has made an impact on Talia. She gets to her feet and shakes her head. She doesn't want to show that she's any the worse for wear. Talia takes the free kick. Distance shouldn't be a problem. And now Isabella comes running past. What an aggressive move from her. Talia takes the chance and slips a handball to her. Isabella is at full speed now and doesn't waste time to put it through. Another goal to the Scorpions! Kicked by Isabella, a back who has taken defence into attack. Coach Brenda will be pleased to see that because it gives her team some breathing space. The Ravens are in for a fight.

The siren sounds and Coach Brenda sprints onto the ground. She quickly gathers the girls around her and prepares them for the last quarter.

I suspect this game might go down to the wire. Coach Brenda has told the girls to expect the Ravens to throw everything at them in this last quarter. 'Keep talking to each other. Don't get rattled and get ahead of yourself. Simply continue to play our game.'

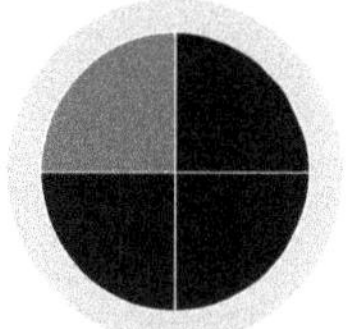

FINAL QUARTER

Maddy, the Ravens' best player, roves the ball well in the middle of the ground. She finds it and accelerates away. Here comes the Ravens' answer to that last goal from the Scorpions. Maddy kicks deep into their forward zone. Ravens forwards are on song here. Their full forward, Kaitlyn, comes out to meet it. Tracks it. Traps it. One bounce. She's looking for space. Isabella launches into a tackle on Kaitlyn and, by the look of it, that tackle took it out of the Ravens' forward. She gets a hand to the ball but it rolls over the boundary line for a throw-in. Heidi soars and gets a beautiful backward tap. Beth reads it best and collects the tap out. Beth handballs and experience wins the day as Bec grabs the footy with one hand. This is great defence from the Scorpions. But can they turn defence into attack? Can they get through this Ravens wall?

Bec kicks across goal to Hannah and who does she find but Isabella who has left her opponent way up ground. She is completely in the clear. Isabella goes for a run again. One bounce. Two bounces. Third bounce with attack coming at her from Maddy. Isabella launches a very big bomb from 50 metres out. It sails over the heads of players. It bounces, rolls, bounces, skews to the right, Ravens defenders are desperate. But they lose the race and it gets there! It's another goal to the newest team in the competition.

Looks like Isabella got another dream goal without moving to full forward after all. And there's her grandmother Lizzie clapping wildly. The Scorpions' crowd can smell victory. They're hoping for the siren. And there it goes! The Scorpions have won their first game.

Coach Brenda sprints out onto the ground with a huge smile, hugging each of her players as she goes. What a game! Andy is beside himself, high-fiving the parents around him. Brenda gathers the girls in the middle of the ground, tears in her eyes, praising them for a great team performance. All that hard work has paid off. The Scorpions Under 14 Girls can't believe their first win and belt out a rousing chorus of their team song. And why not after such a thumping win!

GO SCORPIONS!!

WIN

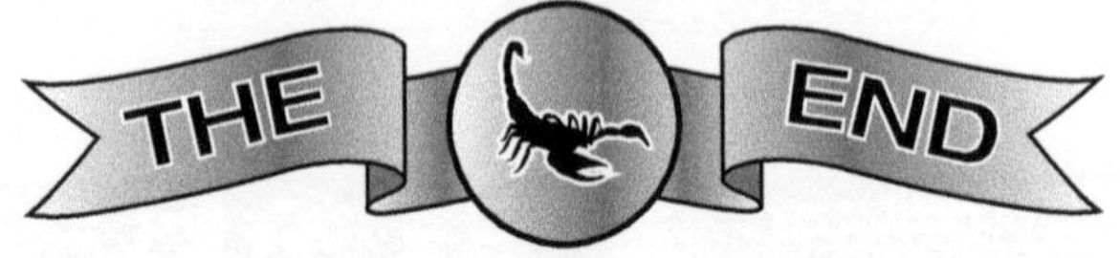

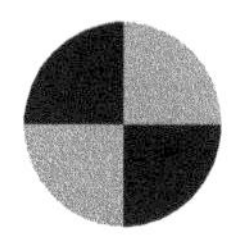

You decided that Ivy kicks a torpedo

Ivy takes a good long look at the goals. The siren sounds for the end of the quarter so this kick better work. Before the siren, a few of her teammates were making leads but they haven't seen what she intends to do. Holding the ball in that slightly slanted angle, Ivy runs in, drops the ball onto her foot perfectly and there it goes in that wonderful arc of a torpedo – sometimes known as a barrel – and does not diverge from its spiralling trajectory, spinning the whole time. And . . .
hold your breath . . . going and going . . .
and through it goes, sailing over the heads of forwards and defenders alike, straight through the middle.
Extraordinary! How often do you see a torpedo at this level?! Ivy is very happy and relieved to see it go through because

if it hadn't, there might've been a bit of criticism of her selection of kick. Years of kick-to-kick in the backyard with her dad and brothers had taught her how to do the perfect torpedo.

Scorpions are 11 points up but they seem to be a bit nervous. They probably can't believe they're in front with one quarter to go. Coach Brenda has told the girls to keep talking to each other. To keep communicating. Just before the siren goes for the start you can see the Scorpions' various zones talking to each other: defenders, forwards and on-ballers. All are encouraging each other. Hannah, Isabella and Beth. Zoe, Talia and Thao.

Heidi with her on-ballers. Grace, Ruby and Ava. The Scorpions are on a mission to win.

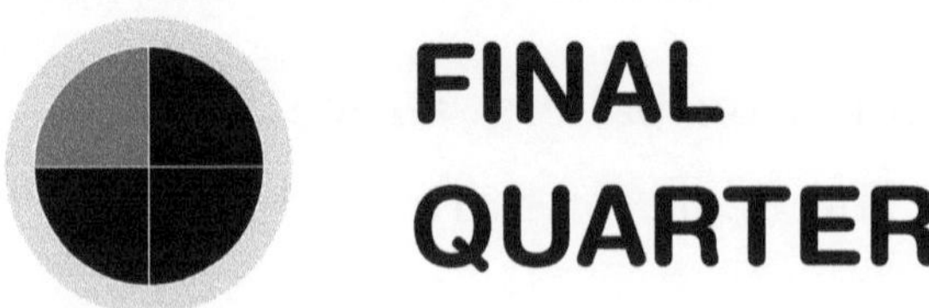

FINAL QUARTER

The umpire holds up the ball, blows her whistle. Heidi leaps like she has springs in her boots, but Ravens steal it away. Onto their Centre to see if she can move it forward. And she does with a good kick towards Ravens' goals. Chandra marks it in defence and sends it back with a well-disciplined kick to Emma. You can always recognise her – never without a helmet. Good work there. Emma slows the play and puts it further downfield, but a Ravens back is there to chop it off. She tries to get on with it but a heap of players converge. Falling over each other. The ball bobbles around, waiting for somebody to do something with it. A player underneath it all – can't see who it is – taps it away. Ruby kicks short and straight into Heidi's hands. The short kick was unselfish as Ruby could've shot for goal. A good idea considering how strong the breeze is. Heidi shoots for goal but only manages a behind.

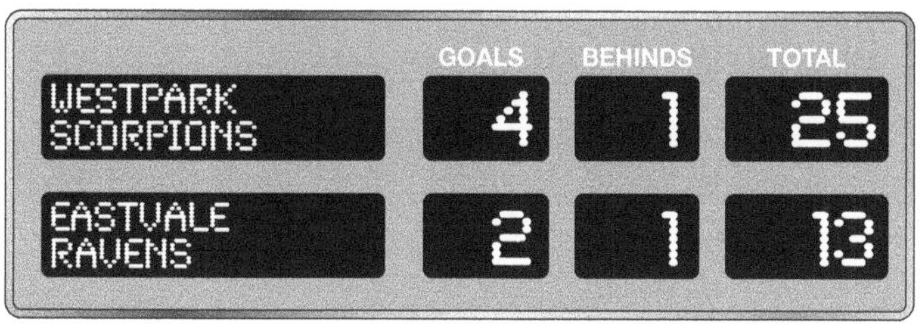

The Scorpions gather around Heidi and tell her not to worry. 'You'll get it next time,' they say. Ravens kick out to a teammate in the back pocket. In turn, she goes back across goal but Zoe cuts it off! A dreadful mistake by the Ravens. Heidi has a few words with Zoe, no doubt warning her about the breeze. Zoe gives her a thumbs-up. From only a minor angle and only 15 out, it goes right through the big sticks. And even though the crowd has sounded like rain on a tin roof the whole of the game, the noise now goes up a notch. Listen to that! There's nothing like a Captain's goal.

Scorpions appear to be in control of this game, and Ravens are being made to work hard for very little reward. In open territory, there's a race for the ball. Jasmine is off the interchange so she's got plenty of steam. First one there will get a huge advantage. Ravens win the foot race. One of the Ravens' better players, Maddy, collects the footy and keeps running. She reaches the 20 metre line on a slight angle, doesn't look to pass it off and goes for it. Only a behind. She tried desperately to lift her team, but a behind isn't going to do it.

Hannah kicks out to Isabella who fumbles the ball. Very strange to see her do that. It gives the Ravens' forward, Kaitlyn, a chance to pick it up and blast away at goals, but again, only a behind. Ravens are giving their all, but no chocolate box so far and time is certainly running out for this experienced team.

This time, Isabella kicks out straight to Hannah. No fumbling there. Then a long handball to Jasmine who's in the clear. Here's an opportunity which Jasmine takes. She wheels around and is away. Scorpions are lining up for this ball. Good kick down the line. Should've been a nice safe mark but it's out of bounds on the full. Free to the Ravens. A Ravens player takes the chance and kicks into the centre. They have to take chances if they're to get back into this game.

Once more we see Jasmine arrive, ball at her feet. No kicking in danger there since the Scorpions have gained several metres. Here comes Talia up forward to meet the ball. There's hugely growing confidence amongst the Scorpions now. Talia brings it down to ground where Thao is front and centre. Thao runs around two Ravens opponents, which is a pretty cheeky thing to do. Looks to handball, decides against it and does it all by herself. Goal! Wow, Thao! Unbelievable. Siren sounds and the Scorpions have whipped the Ravens into submission with a whopping 22-point win.

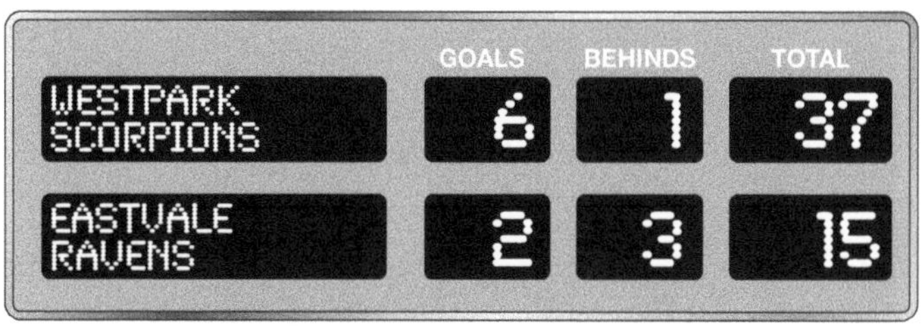

The Scorpions can't believe it. They would never have imagined this victory. There is laughter and tears of joy as they rush to each other and are joined by their supporters. Heidi, Poppy, Ava and Talia are in a group hug. Quickly, Ivy, Zoe and Bec join them. Isabella and Hannah race in and before you know it, all the Scorpions pile onto each other celebrating their first win in the comp. Parents take photos of this great scene. The Scorpions' first win!

Thunderous clapping and cheering follows the girls into the rooms and a special three cheers for Ivy and her torpedo, which opened the floodgates for a huge Scorpions win. What a day to remember!

WIN

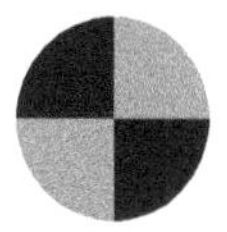

You decided that Ivy doesn't go for a torpedo.

Looks like Ivy is having second thoughts. She changes the way she's holding the leather. The distance will certainly test her. Instead, she decides on a big drop punt, which holds up in the air, almost like it's floating. It is not going to make the distance though. A Ravens full back comes from the side and punches it through for a behind.

End of the quarter for half-time. That goal would have put the Scorpions up by 11 points, but nothing doing.

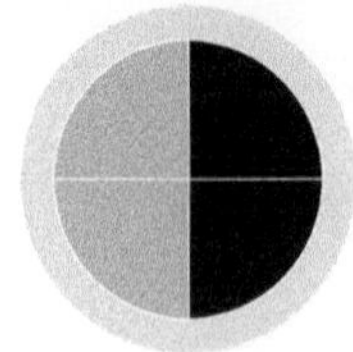

HALF-TIME

As the team jogs off the ground, Coach Brenda runs out onto the field and gives Ivy a consoling pat as she passes her. Now Ivy wishes she tried the torpedo.

Coach and Andy are worried about how the team will run out the rest of the game. Anna tells the girls to get a rub down if they need it while Andy reminds them to rehydrate. They're worried that the girls' legs won't hold up in this absolutely exhausting game. Ravens are known for their never-say-die attitude. The coach urges her girls on, telling them that they're even. That the Ravens are still in the game, only one kick behind. 'Even if you're feeling exhausted, I want you to keep going. Try and make the Ravens crack. They're already a bit concerned about us and our effort. All right, all hands in!'

The team bunches together and yells, ***'SCORPIONS!!'***

THIRD QUARTER

The Ravens' ruck, Rose, takes the ball out of the contest and kicks big out from the middle. Zoe takes a desperate mark in defence. Hannah copped a whack in that pack but play goes on. Hannah's asking the umpire why she didn't get a free, but she doesn't get an answer with the ball coming straight back into the Ravens' forward zone. Players pile in as the ball sails high through the air. Isabella grabs it, loses it. Ravens chasing it out near the boundary. Matilda is in the hunt. Can she get there in time? A Raven slides in and takes it over the line.

At the throw-in, it seems like most of the Scorpions are down in defence. The Ravens are now stepping up their work rate. Again, the footy comes close to the boundary but it stays in and Matilda and Elly fight for the ball against some desperate Ravens. Somehow, a Ravens player squeezes out a kick that lands close to their point post. The Ravens are keeping it in play. The ball is in mid-air. Out of the blue, Kaitlyn comes in from the side, gets boot to ball and through for a goal. Scores are tied! Now the Scorpions know what scoreboard pressure means.

The game begins again just as the siren sounds for the end of the quarter. Coach Brenda runs to the middle and quickly gathers the girls in a huddle, trying to keep their nerves under control.

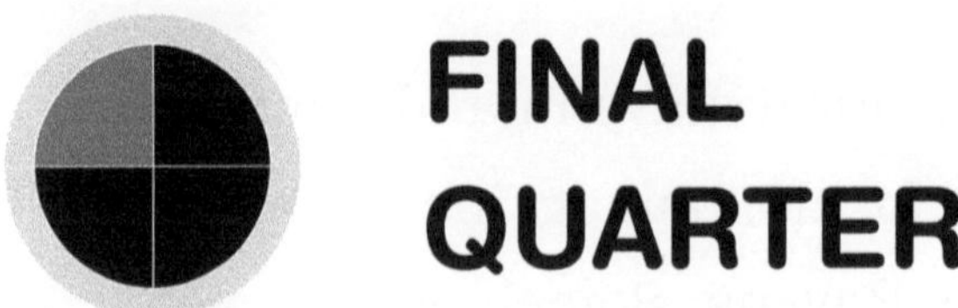

FINAL QUARTER

Talia is in the ruck while Heidi moves down forward where the Scorpions need to concentrate their efforts. The backs are holding up well. Talia wins the hit-out, but it goes straight into the hands of the Ravens outside player, who doesn't waste time driving it into their forward line where it is marked by Isabella's direct opponent. The forward holds up the ball and shows it to Isabella who has beaten her all day. We'll see how her kick for goal goes. Close, close to the goal post but it sneaks through and it's another goal to the Ravens.

Scorpions gather in the middle and organise themselves. This time, Rose takes the ball out of the air, handballs forward to a running player who gets to 45 metres out and launches it towards goal. Will it go through? Yes, but only for a behind.

Isabella doesn't muck around at the kick out. She baulks around the Ravens defender on the mark and sends it out to the wing where Ava is waiting. Ava runs around and then backwards and short passes to Ivy who gets it to Elly on a lead. Elly keeps on running and decides to go for it. But no score at all and no box of chocolates. Maybe that ankle of hers was a factor. The crowd from both sides are on their feet. There isn't long to go. The Scorpions have to kick two goals to beat the Ravens. Tough ask.

Heidi is back in the ruck and Talia plays deep. A Ravens player kicks very long out to the wing, but Thao makes a great contest. The ball spills out to Ruby who opts to go sideways. Safe mark by Emma! Teammates and the crowd urge her to play on. Emma doesn't panic, deciding not to blaze away. The umpire tells her to play on. Emma finds Grace, who gathers. She runs with the Ravens hot on her tail. Almost gets pinged. Grace handballs over the top to Heidi, who's good in the air as well as on the ground.

Heidi goes for it and suddenly we see Zoe leap magnificently, riding on shoulders, bring it down and land with a thump 15 metres out and directly in front. Her teammates tell her to get going which she does and slots another goal to the Scorpions. How did this game get so hot!?

The game is coming right down to the wire. All players are totally dedicated, totally alert and on their toes. Ball-up and the Scorpions go at it. Who would have believed this game would turn out like this? Bec, Zoe and Emma are putting it all on the line. Zoe wrestles for the ball, hoping for the best. It looks like a holding free to Zoe but it goes unnoticed. Umpires are not too keen on giving free kicks at stages like this in a game. A scrambled kick out of the centre by the Ravens miraculously falls into the hands of a Ravens player. The siren can't be far away now. She sees her ruck is free and gets it to Rose with a short, accurate kick. But no! Beth cuts it off. And there goes the siren. The Scorpions are beaten by one point. Can you believe that?!

The Scorpions team drops to its knees as one. Zoe is devastated and cries on Holly's shoulder. Coach Brenda walks from player to player telling them they might've been beaten, but they can hold their heads up high. From now on, no team can take the Scorpions Girls for granted.

Back in the change rooms, Isabella leads three cheers for Brenda, Andy and Anna. A close loss for their first game in the comp against last year's Premiers is a top effort, say a few of the parents. A bittersweet result for the girls, almost a win but better than a flogging, Matilda admits. Brenda gathers the girls and quietly says, 'Bring on Game Two. All right, all hands in!'

The team bunches together and yells, ***'SCORPIONS!!'***

	GOALS	BEHINDS	TOTAL
WESTPARK SCORPIONS	4	1	25
EASTVALE RAVENS	4	2	26

LOSS

Acknowledgements

Many thank-yous to the footy tragics who helped us by sharing their experiences and insights. Thanks to our nephew Andrew Hyde, for the loads of footage and stills; our great-niece Heidi and her teammates; and another young footballer, family friend, Isabella, for dealing with our never-ending questions about her experiences in the game. Our hard-working editors Abigail and Robyn never let us off the hook with their own set of never-ending questions which made our little book all the better. Finally for the great photo on the cover, thanks for permission from the photographer, Scott Moorhen.